What to Do When Your Family Loses Its Home

Rachel Lynette

PowerKiDS press

New York

Published in 2010 by The Rosen Publishing Group, Inc.
29 East 21st Street, New York, NY 10010

First Edition

Editor: Joanne Randolph
Book Design: Julio Gil
Photo Researcher: Jessica Gerweck

Photo Credits: Cover Altrendo Images/Getty Images; pp. 4, 6, 10, 12, 18, 20 Shutterstock.com; p. 8 © Jeff Greenberg/age fotostock; p. 14 John Moore/Getty Images; p. 16 Joe Raedle/Getty Images.

Library of Congress Cataloging-in-Publication Data

Lynette, Rachel.
  What to do when your family loses its home / Rachel Lynette. — 1st ed.
    p. cm. — (Let's work it out)
  Includes index.
  ISBN 978-1-4358-9339-9 (library binding) — ISBN 978-1-4358-9766-3 (pbk.) —
ISBN 978-1-4358-9767-0 (6-pack)
  1. Homeless families—United States—Juvenile literature. 2. Shelters for the homeless—United States—Juvenile literature. I. Title.
  HV4505.L96 2010
  362.50973—dc22
                          2009023066

Manufactured in the United States of America

CPSIA Compliance Information: Batch #WW10PK: For Further Information contact Rosen Publishing, New York, New York at 1-800-237-9932

Contents

Having to move to a new home can seem scary and make you feel sad, but your parents are doing what is best for your family.

A Moving Story

Brendan lived in a nice house with his younger sister and his parents. Then Brendan's father lost his job. He tried hard to get another job, but he could not find one. Brendan's mother still had her job, but she did not make enough money for everything the family needed. Soon, Brendan's parents fell behind on their **mortgage** payments. Brendan's family had to sell their house.

Brendan's family lost their home. A family that loses its home must find another place to live. If your family loses its home, things may be hard for a while, but soon your family will find a new home.

Your parents may find that they are spending more money than they make. They may need to cut costs by moving to a cheaper home.

What Happened?

There are many reasons a family might lose its home. If a parent loses her job and cannot find another one, she may not be able to pay the rent or mortgage. A parent could also become ill and be unable to work.

A family may also lose its home if the parents divorce. When parents divorce, they have to pay for two places to live instead of one. Sometimes the parent who takes care of the children cannot **afford** to keep the same house.

Sometimes a family loses its home because of a fire, flood, or other natural disaster. In 2005, many people lost their homes to Hurricane Katrina.

You may miss your old home at first, but the new place will soon feel like home. This girl felt better after she painted her new room.

Downsizing

If your family loses its home because the payments for it are too high, you may have to move to a smaller house or apartment. You may not be able to bring all your furniture or all your toys with you. You may not be able to bring your pets, either. You may have to share your bedroom with another family member. You may have to change schools.

Moving to a new home is a big change. It can seem scary or make you feel sad. What can you do to make things better? **Decorating** your new room can help you feel more at home. Are there kids in your new neighborhood? Making new friends will help, too.

Living with grandparents can be a great way to get to know them better. Tell them about your interests, and ask them about theirs.

All in the Family

One of the best things about being part of a family is that families help each other. Your family is much bigger than just your mom, dad, brothers, and sisters. You have other **relatives**, too, such as grandparents, aunts, uncles, and cousins. If your family loses its home, some of your relatives might help out by letting your family live with them for a little while.

Jenny's family moved in with her grandparents. At first, Jenny felt strange living in their house. Then Jenny's grandma taught her to knit. She told Jenny stories about when she was a little girl. Jenny still missed her old house, but she enjoyed growing closer to her grandma.

Playing outside gives everyone a break from a crowded house. You could build a snowman in the winter or play tag on warm days.

Too Many People!

Living with relatives can be fun, but it can also be **stressful**. You may have to follow new rules. You may feel like there are too many people in the house. How can you make things better?

When a lot of people live in a small space, things tend to get messy. Adults often feel stressed when the house is messy. You can help by not leaving your things around. Think of ways you can help, then follow through and do them.

Another thing that makes adults feel stressed is too much noise. Can you talk in a quiet voice? Can you walk instead of run? Small changes can make a big difference!

This family is living in a shelter for now, but they know that having a family that loves you is more important than where you live.

A Shelter Can Help

Sometimes a family that loses its home cannot move in with relatives. Families who cannot move in with relatives may have to live in a shelter. A shelter is a place where people who do not have homes can stay. This may sound scary or **embarrassing**. Just remember, you will be there only for a little while.

There is not much room in a shelter. You will not be able to bring many things there. Sometimes a shelter may not have enough room for your whole family. If that happens, your family may have to split up for a while. However, you will always be with one of your parents and you will all be back together soon.

Here a family is getting food at a shelter. Try to think of shelter life as an adventure and make the most of it.

Life in a Shelter

Most families stay in a shelter for only a few weeks or months. Your family might sleep in a big room with a lot of beds. In some shelters, each family is given a room where they sleep and keep their clothes. There might be a place where everyone in the shelter can watch TV and play games.

Life in a shelter is different from life at home. There are rules that everyone must follow. Everyone in a shelter gets up at the same time. People eat meals together. There may be a bedtime for all children in the shelter. These rules make the shelter run smoothly.

Soon your family will move into a new home, as this family is. It will be hard work, but your family can do it if they stick to a plan.

Back on Your Feet

Whether you are living with relatives or you are staying in a shelter, your parents will be working hard to get your family back on its feet. One of the **benefits** of being in a shelter is that your family will work with a **caseworker**. The caseworker will help your parents make a plan to get better jobs, save money, and find a **permanent** place to live. If you are living with family, your parents will come up with a plan on their own.

Following the plan will be a lot of work for your parents. They may need to learn new skills to find a new job. They may spend a lot of time looking for a house or apartment. It will be worth the hard work, though, when your family moves into its new home!

No matter what is going on in your life, friends are important. It is okay to have fun even if your family is going through a hard time.

At School

Moving to a relative's house or a shelter may mean that you have to go to a new school. You may feel **ashamed** or embarrassed that your family has lost its home. You may not want anyone at your new school to know. Try to remember that it is not your fault that your family needed to move. You did not do anything wrong.

If other children tease you, try not to be mean back. Can you walk away instead? Can you tell a teacher? Can you make friends with children who are nice to you? Moving to a new place has not changed who you are. Finding true friends who care about you will help you feel better.

Talk It Over

You likely have a lot of feelings about losing your home. You might miss your old home. You may feel scared, angry, sad, or embarrassed that you need to move to a smaller, cheaper place. It can help to talk to your family about your feelings. Your parents might be able to tell you things that will make you feel better.

If you are feeling very unhappy, you may want to talk to a family **counselor**. A family counselor can help you and your parents cope, or deal, with your feelings. She may also have ideas about how to deal with problems at school. Talking to a counselor can really help!

Glossary

afford (uh-FAWRD) To have enough money to pay for something.

ashamed (uh-SHAYMD) Uncomfortable because of something you did.

benefits (BEH-neh-fits) Programs that help people pay for things they need.

caseworker (KAYS-wer-ker) A person who helps people who are having trouble dealing with their problems.

counselor (KOWN-seh-ler) Someone who talks with people about their feelings and problems.

decorating (DEH-kuh-rayt-ing) Adding objects that make something prettier or more interesting.

embarrassing (em-BAR-us-ing) Causing feelings of shame.

mortgage (MAWR-gij) An agreement to use a building or piece of land as security for a loan. If the loan is not paid back, the lender gets to keep the property.

permanent (PER-muh-nint) Lasting for a long time.

relatives (REH-luh-tivz) Kin, or people in the same family who share the same blood.

stressful (STRES-ful) Causing worry or bad feelings.

Index

Web Sites

Due to the changing nature of Internet links, PowerKids Press has developed an online list of Web sites related to the subject of this book. This site is updated regularly. Please use this link to access the list:
www.powerkidslinks.com/lwio/home/